Letter To Larry

A play
Based on the life of Vivien Leigh

by
Donald Macdonald

Playdead Press

Published by Playdead Press 2012

A CIP catalogue record for this book is available from the British Library.

ISBN 978-0-9572859-0-3

Playdead Press
www.playdeadpress.com

Acknowledgements: Anne Edward's wonderful biography of Vivien Leigh has been most helpful, as has Vivien by Alexander Walker. I have also been assisted by Laurence Olivier's, Confessions of an Actor. Letter To Larry features lyrics of "A marvelous party" by Noel Coward, and lines from "A Streetcar Named Desire" by Tennesee Williams.

With grateful thanks to Susie Lindeman.

Donald Macdonald is an award-winning screenwriter, and novelist. His other plays include Hot Taps, Seasons, and Boulevard Play. His first play Caravan is one of Australia's most successful and endearing stage comedies. He has performed his solo show, The Gospel of St. John, around the world.

Letter to Larry was first performed as part of a Jubilee Preview season on 6th June 2012, at the Jermyn Street Theatre, London. Presented in association with Cheepuk. The cast was as follows:

Vivien Leigh:	Susie Lindeman

Director:	Donald Macdonald
Lighting Design	Chris Page
Sound Design	Michael Roberts

Please note the stage version differs slightly from published version.

JERMYN STREET THEATRE

Letter To Larry

by

Donald Macdonald

CHARACTERS:

VIVIEN LEIGH

ACT ONE

Scene one

Time: Saturday 19th May, 1960.
The star dressing room in the Helen Hayes theatre, New York.

A dressing table with mirror and lights is downstage centre and faces the audience, so when the actress looks into the mirror she is looking at the audience. There is a couch, with a small table alongside, well stocked with champagne, wine and spirits. On another table, a phone and a gramophone. Framed photographs also sit on the tables. The room is filled with flowers... A door left, leads to the stage; another door, upstage centre, leads to a bathroom. A screen is placed by that door. On it hang the different props, to be used by the actress. Hats. Furs etc.

OFF: *(the SOUND of tumultuous applause. CHEERS and BRAVOS!)*

The door opens and ***VIVIEN LEIGH*** *enters, closes the door quickly and leans against it, trying to get her breath. Her mood is a mixture of exultation and panic. She is dressed in the costume she wears for the final act of the play "A Duel of Angels."*

OFF: *The APPLAUSE continues.*

VIVIEN *pours herself a gin and tonic and drinks quickly. She removes her costume and puts on a robe. She tops up her drink, carries it to her dressing table and stares at her reflection in the mirror. She is of course, heavily made up in a theatrical way and looks beautiful. She has been a very beautiful woman in youth and is still beautiful in her middle forties, but life has taken its price from her, and the beauty is fading. She listens to the last of the APPLAUSE. Silence.*
She puts her head briefly in her hands. After a moment, she lights a cigarette and inhales deeply, coughs, then places the cigarette in an ashtray as she prepares to take off her makeup.
She speaks it is in a distinctive, purring voice with a crystal-clear English accent.

VIVIEN: Judy Garland said applause made you feel loved. Nothing is more exhilarating than a packed house telling you how much they love you. Then, you go home alone. *(She sips her gin thoughtfully, and picks up a newspaper folded neatly on her dressing table. She reads aloud.)* Lady Olivier wishes to say that Sir Laurence has asked for a divorce in order to marry Miss Joan Plowright. She will naturally do whatever he wishes." *(She begins to take off her makeup.)*

Tonight, when I especially needed them, this audience was wonderful. For a moment I did feel loved. For a moment I forgot the pain. You will never know, Larry, what courage it took for me to go out on that stage tonight. I stood in the wings and shook with fear. When I went on, I froze centre-stage. The actor's worst nightmare. For one dreadful moment I completely lost the character of Paola. I was Vivien Leigh and I was terrified. Trembling. Speechless. Then the house rose to its feet and gave me a standing ovation. Dear Jack Merivale stood aside to let me know it was all for me. That wonderful, loving applause saved me. *(Smiles)* Standing ovations have been happening quite often in New York, which is nice. As you well know, Larry, I have always loved an audience. I suppose that's why I act. *(Pause)* I love people. I like giving pleasure My Mother always insisted on pleasing others before yourself. "When you are a guest at a party," Gertrude said, "do whatever the hostess wants to please her. And when you are the hostess, do what the guests want to please them." It never occurred to me that I might please myself. I only ever wanted to please you, Larry...

She again inhales on her cigarette. Still wiping her face, she goes to a telephone by the couch. Picks up the receiver, puts it down.

VIVIEN: No messages. You haven't rung. If I telephone, you won't answer.

She returns to her dressing table, and picks up a letter.

VIVIEN: I suppose in some dark part of my soul, I was expecting your letter, but when it finally came, it deeply distressed me. I had the shakes. I couldn't stop crying. *(Pause)* No doubt you are appalled I let the cat out of the bag to the press. And on the day of your fifty third birthday! Happy birthday, dear Larry.

She raises her glass in a mock toast to him. She continues removing her makeup.

VIVIEN: It's the first time I haven't got you anything, and you know how I enjoy buying gifts for someone I love. *(Pause)* I'm writing you a letter. I tremble as I write it, afraid of what I might say, afraid if I don't say it. I write it over and over in my head, reciting it like the lines of a play. My farewell speech to you. *(Pause)* I write so many letters to everyone, yet I can't find the right words for the one I love most. But then I have loved you in a way that is beyond words. *(Pause)* I wonder what <u>Joan</u> gave you for your birthday? I hardly think that quaint little thing has very much taste. No doubt you will help her to acquire it as I did for you. Anyway, you forgot my birthday. November 5th. You had never missed it before. How could you forget Guy Fawkes's night?

"Mummy, why are people making so much noise outside?"
"It's your birthday, darling. When you were born, the evening sky exploded with fireworks!"

Well, that's what Gertrude always said. Did she ever please herself, I wonder? She once threw a dinner party and invited all Daddy's ex-mistresses. Oh, she was strong, my Mother. She had to be, to cope with Daddy's infidelities. Divorce was out of the question so Mother found her solace in the Catholic Church. I wish I had her faith. Especially tonight. But I never became the Catholic, Gertrude wanted me to be. I do still keep the notebooks of St. Therese of Liseux by my bed. I was given a very good Catholic education.

She is thoughtful as she remembers the past. The lights begin to change.

VIVIEN: The Convent school at Roehampton, outside London. Vivien Mary Hartley was the youngest child they ever accepted. Only six and half, so small and frail. *(She smokes, and coughs)* With a weak chest...

(Pause) You know the story, Larry, you've heard all my stories. But as I consider my reply to your letter, and of course I must reply, I will reply, I do find myself dwelling on the past. Trying to make some sense of it... Going back...

Lights change. On a screen behind ***VIVIEN****, is the Convent of the Sacred Heart. Music. As* ***VIVIEN*** *talks she becomes for moments a little girl again...*

VIVIEN: We have come in a taxi. It's not far from London, Mother assures me, but so frighteningly far from India where I was born. I stand in the cold, unwelcoming courtyard under swirling grey clouds. Poor, frightened little creature. So very afraid. Shivering in this bleak, cold place. I am so cold. I hate the cold. Where is the sun? I have always lived in the sun... We would go up into the hills, into the warmth of the golden sunlight. The elegant ladies, handsome officers, like Daddy, riding beautiful horses, delicious strange foods! I can still smell them! *(She takes a deep pleasurable breath.)* I open my eyes to this grey courtyard. The Mother Superior hovers over me like some great black bird, gripping me in her strong hand. I am afraid she will fly away with me. Mother looks almost cheerful.

"Vivien, this is the right decision for your future!!"

Tears are wasted on her. Can't you see my heart is breaking? Don't leave me!! Please don't leave me, Mummy! Don't leave me! Don't leave me, Larry…

*A moment as **VIVIEN** collects herself.*

VIVIEN: My mother returns to the sun. You were my sun, Larry. And you have left me. I didn't see Gertrude again for two years. India for many years. I wonder if that first awful morning started my troubles? Do you think so, Larry? I wonder when I will see you again. I write this letter to beg you to see me…

Music. A bell rings. On the screen is a school dormitory with rows of beds. Lights change to suggest another time.

VIVIEN: I sleep in a dormitory with twenty other girls up at six thirty every morning to the Angelus Bell. We dress behind a curtain, and bathe always wearing a shift. No-one must see our bodies. Perhaps that explains my strange urge to remove all my clothes whenever I am mad. "Wash away our sins!" we chant. What sins could we possibly have at that age? There are girls from all over Europe, but I have come from India so I am considered "foreign". I am special. Special, and alone in the holidays when all the girls return to their families. Nobody invites me anywhere. I am left with the nuns and Mother Superior, who gives me a kitten for a companion. I was grateful to her for that. And she taught me to always have clean underwear. I did finally make a friend to comfort me in my loneliness. You know how important friendship is to me, Larry. I treasure my friends. I am very loyal, Larry. Maureen O'Sullivan was my first friend in the Convent.

"I'm going to be an actress, Maureen!"
"Why on earth would you want to be an Actress?"
"Not any kind of Actress. A great one!"
"Good for you. I'm going to be a pilot."

Fifteen years later, Maureen and I acted together in the same film! Then she acted with Tarzan. How very strange life can be!

"Vivien, I hope you have tribulation. It will do you a lot of good. Your best friends should wish it for you."
"Sister, my Mummy and Daddy jolly well don't wish that! And they are my very, very, very best friends! I think it is horrid of you to say that. I jolly well won't give myself any trouble or tribulation or whatever you call the beastly thing…"

Lights up in the dressing room. ***VIVIEN*** *looks up to Heaven.*

VIVIEN: God, if you are speaking to Sister, tell her the Tribulation has arrived. If she is up there. She might not be. She was a cranky old cow. *(Pause)* I feel safe sitting in a dressing room. I think it is the only place I do feel safe. Every night I come in here an hour and a half before curtain time. I'm so afraid of forgetting my lines; I have to say the part over to myself. Not aloud, just to myself, as I slowly become this other woman, Paola, in Duel of Angels. Hot tempered and passionate like me. Yet sometimes the truth of the lines I speak fills me with dread. The dread was very real tonight. You must never show it, that's the discipline. *(In Larry's voice)* "I'm proud of you! You are such a disciplined actress!" You once said that to me in rehearsal. I am not disciplined at all in the real world. I'm a Scorpio. They eat themselves up and burn themselves out. I say what I think and don't pretend, and I am prepared to accept the consequences of my actions. At least, I thought I was. *(She pulls off the wig.)* Now, the wig comes off I am myself again.

She has short brown hair, cut in the rather matronly fashion of the time. She stares at herself in the mirror, and smokes. She has finished removing her makeup. She takes off her robe and pulls on a black skirt, with a cream blouse.

VIVIEN: Would you believe me, Larry, if I told you I can hardly remember what I said to the Press? I was in such a state of shock after I received your letter that I picked up the telephone, and I really didn't know what I was saying. *(Harshly)* Well, what did you expect? A discreet, understanding reply. *(She picks up the letter)* How can I reply to this! I don't even know how to begin. Do I call you Darling Larry, or dear Larry? Or dear Sir Laurence Olivier?

She sits down at the dressing table, combs her hair. Her face without makeup is still beautiful, but she is older, and full of sad desperation. She begins to freshen up her makeup as she talks.

VIVIEN: I write little notes to Jack Merivale all the time, even though he is in the next dressing room. He is not like you. He doesn't stir my soul. But I feel he has woken me from a fever. He is a good man. I write to tell him how grateful I am for his goodness. Do you know I wrote him a letter on the fourteenth of May, but I mistakenly dated it the Nineteenth. Did I have a strange premonition? Some sort of ESP? The 19th

May, 1960. The day I receive a long and very moving letter from my husband, Sir Laurence Olivier, asking me for a divorce. *(Mimics Olivier's voice as she reads)* "Joan and I are very much in love." Joan Plowright. She of the new generation at the Royal Court that you wanted so much to be part of to prove yourself once again. To hold back the years. Nothing can hold them back. Nothing. My beautiful, shining, brilliant, darling Larry...

...I loved you better than I loved myself. It doesn't matter if you don't hold me in your arms with passion. Hold me gently like a loving friend. That would be enough... *(She continues reading-again mimicking Olivier)* "Joan is asking for a divorce from her husband, and after much great soul-searching, I am asking you to release us both from an untenable relationship..." Untenable. What a horrid word. It sounds vaguely filthy. As though we had done something disgusting! We loved each other! We are the golden couple! The glittering, golden, golden... *(She breaks off)* You shared my youth, and my love, and my dreams. So many memories only you can share. I did everything to please you!! It was all for you! My illness leaves me so confused. I feel helpless like a child. I just want your comfort. I need your comfort! You even ask me to sell the house where we shared the happiest times of our lives! How could you ask me to sell Notley, the only home I ever really had? If you had an ounce of sensitivity or understanding you must know what that would do to me?

You want to move on. I can't live there without you. The memories would rise up and choke me.

You didn't even want to be with me for Christmas, going off blithely to the States, abandoning me to the kindness of friends. Noel Coward carried me off to Switzerland, and bless him, managed to keep the press away. Noellie was shocked. He always hoped we would stay together...

He and I played charades. A lot. Noel only wants to play because he is always the best. *(Pause)* Not a very jolly Christmas. My father, Ernest, died on the eighteenth of December. Perhaps the news didn't reach you? Or were you enjoying yourself so much you couldn't spare the time for even a sympathy note? Ernest was seventy five. Still so handsome and pleasure loving. Wilful, just like me. I feel his death is some dreadful omen. Everything is slipping away. I try to hold onto what little dignity I have, but you leave me with nothing. *(Bright)* Gertrude, however, is better than ever! She looks quite sixteen! She's opened a beauty business and started behaving, as if she were the real "star" of the family. We were never close, but strangely now I lean on her. *(Pause)* I am not close to my own daughter.

She picks up a framed photograph of Olivier, which sits on her dressing table.

VIVIEN: I still keep your photograph by my bed. And I carry one in my bag. *(Pause)* The last time you actually talked to me, it was as if you were speaking politely to a stranger. You don't want to be bothered with me. I'm too much trouble. I'm sick, Larry! I have a mental illness! I need you! At this moment in my life I need you desperately!

She pours herself another drink.

VIVIEN: I'm drinking far too much. I worry I am entering one of my manic phases. Why can't you love me as I am? I won't give you up. I won't…

She examines her face in the mirror.

VIVIEN: But I have lost you, as surely as I have lost my youth…

She moves away from the mirror and puts on a black jacket.

VIVIEN: A friend was with me when I received your letter. After she had managed to calm me, she asked me what I was going to do. "Whatever Larry wants me to do," I said.

Lights fade.
End Scene One

Act One
Scene Two

Three days later.
*In the spotlight a young **VIVIEN** is remembered, wearing the black suit, to which is added a fur, and a hat. On the screen behind, we see the Savoy Grill. Voices. Music under.*

***VIVIEN** stretches out a hand, smiling her beguiling, kittenish smile to great effect.*

VIVIEN: "How do you do, Mr. Olivier. My name is Vivien Leigh. I saw you as Tony Cavendish in A Theatre Royal. It was a superb performance..."

For a moment, she enjoys remembering.

VIVIEN: I will never forget that first moment I saw you on stage. Dark eyes, slim hips, very tight trousers. Shirt open to the waist, leaping from a balcony like Douglas Fairbanks. The sexual energy burst out of you. And aroused in me a sexuality I had never experienced. I loved you from that moment. We are finally introduced at the Savoy Grill. Of course, I know you often dine there, so I have blackmailed my escort into bringing me. You're dining with your wife, Jill Esmond. Pretty little thing. An actress, but also the daughter of a prominent theatrical family. You've married well. I smile my most beguiling smile, and I grasp your hand. You greet me casually, but I see something in your eyes. Something unguarded. You've shaved off your little moustache. My escort, sensing something I'm sure, is quite rude about you.

"What a silly little thing, Larry looks without his lip covering!"
"He looks adorable. He's the sort of man I'd like to marry!"

The spotlight fades, and the lights come up in the same dressing room. The room has been changed so that the dressing table is now stage right and the couch off centre. The older ***VIVIEN*** *has removed the fur and the hat. She* *sits, holding her head. Her mood is numb, at times, strangely childlike, and distant.*

VIVIEN: I've been having one of my lapses. *(Pause)* I can't sleep! Not since your letter three days ago. I lie awake with the words of a reply turning over and over in my mind. In the cold light of morning, I am ashamed because the words I want to say seem so full of self -pity. I know if I write what I feel I will only drive you further away. So I begin again this letter to you...

She stands to look in the mirror.

VIVIEN: A burn on my forehead. How hideous. Why can't I have a decent, clean illness? I've always hated illness of any sort. I never had sympathy with anybody who was ill. You just get on with it and recover! Without fuss.

She pours herself a drink and lights a cigarette. She smokes and coughs. She sits again rolling the glass against her head.

VIVIEN: I never have headaches like this when Dr. Conachy treats me. All my instincts told me to telephone him today. He was the first person to recognise what was wrong with me. "You're ill," he said. "I can help you." And he did. I trust him. I never get headaches like this.

A pause. She smiles a little wickedly.

VIVIEN: My announcement to the press has created a worldwide sensation. Larry, darling, I gather, you are not amused. Waking at nine o'clock, on your birthday of all days, to find the road outside jammed with reporters and photographers. Your secretary ran out hysterically. "No comment!" They had to put dear Joan's understudy on at the next performance of "Rhinoceros." Poor Miss Plowright went into hiding. *(Pause)* The Press call her the blue stockinged darling of the new "vital" theatre. I find this "vital" theatre rather turgid. Yet you, my darling Larry, wanted so much to be part of it, you practically went down on your knees and begged John Osborne to put you in "The Entertainer." I could have played the wife. Things might have been very different if I had! You said I was too beautiful. How I loathe that word .When someone calls me beautiful I want to slap them! I did suggest I wear a rubber mask. I don't think John Osborne cared too much for that suggestion. You didn't want me in the play. You were breaking away from the Establishment, leaving me behind. I went to the Royal Court to watch rehearsals. Do you remember, Larry?

"Vivien, darling, your presence is making me just a little nervous."
"Larry, darling, it never has before!"

(Laughs harshly) When I dared to criticise your performance, George Devine, the Artistic Director ordered me out of the theatre! Miss Leigh was asked not to come back! Joan Plowright played as the daughter for the transfer. "The Entertainer" was one of your greatest achievements. It destroyed our lives.

Pause

VIVIEN: It's coming on again. My manic phase. I've been drinking too much, popping tranquillizers, yet still not sleeping. If only I could sleep! I've never slept much, as you know. Sleep always seems such a waste of time. Now I know sleeplessness is a symptom of my illness. As a child, I never gave any trouble to anyone. Gertrude liked my good manners. I don't know that she ever liked me much. Looking back, I think she was afraid of what might happen to me. Once, in Munich, I was only sixteen, such a beautiful young waiter was serving us and I started flirting.

"You deserve to be kissed!" Gertrude slapped my face. A mental illness is somehow shameful... We were travelling through Europe then. Ernest had made money on the stock-market, and decided the world would be my finishing school. I think the idea secretly appealed to Gertrude even though she argued against it. So at fourteen I was taken out of the Convent, and for the next four years we travelled. Paris, Biarritz, the Italian Riviera, Salzburg, Ireland. I was a young woman of the world. We travelled in luxury, until the money ran out. We had so much money for a long time. Suddenly it was gone. Daddy lost it all.

She pours herself another drink.

VIVIEN: Everything goes so fast. Jack says my nervous energy makes me charismatic as a performer. Dear Jack. He is very loyal. But after today...? *(She continues to roll the glass against her forehead)* He looks at me differently...

Music plays

VIVIEN: From that first meeting at the Savoy, I was convinced you were in love with me. If you weren't, you soon would be! I used to have such wild fantasies in the Convent. Later, when Gertrude and Ernest didn't get on, and I felt like some awful intruder in their world, I would withdraw into a secret world of my own. In my magical, mysterious world, there was always a prince, a masked suitor, who never revealed his identity. When I met you Larry, I knew. I recognised you, you see. You had always been there, waiting for me behind the mask. Of course, there was one small problem. We were both married to other people.

*The Lights change. Music. The sound of a horse clipping along cobbled streets. On the screen a village High Street. The young **VIVIEN** is remembered, stands in a spotlight.*

VIVIEN: February 1932. Standing with my girlfriend in the village high street of Holcombe. A handsome man in a red coat rides past on horseback, and tips his hat.

"That's Leigh Holman, Vivien. What do you think? Isn't he handsome?"

"He looks like Leslie Howard, my favourite actor! The same pale, serious eyes. And that delicious blonde wavy hair…"

"He's thirty one! Quite old for a bachelor!"

"I think he looks the perfect Englishman. I'm going to marry him!"

"He's almost engaged to a girl already!"

"That doesn't matter. He hasn't met me yet"

Prayer and Gertrude's training have given me the confidence not to sit and wait for life. Gertrude told me that when she was carrying me, she stood every day facing the Himalayas, to breathe in its beauty. She willed that same beauty for me. Consequently, I have always believed you can get anything you want if your will is strong enough. Of course, then you have to keep it. Leigh and I are formally introduced at the South Devon Hunt Ball. He takes my hand. When he waltzes me around the room, I feel like the leading actress in my own film...

She waltzes gently to music. Fade.

Lights up on the present. The older ***VIVIEN*** *seated on the couch in her dressing room.*

VIVIEN: Gertrude tried to warn me. "Marriage is a sacred vow, Vivien. I worry about you. You are far too restless." She wanted me to attend Mass, and receive instruction from a Priest on the duties of a Catholic mother. I refused. Anyway, I had begun to question the Church, which amused Daddy, but certainly did not amuse my mother. I assured her she had nothing to worry about. Leigh and I were married on the 20th December, 1932 at St. James's Spanish Place, the Society Church, attended by well-to-do Roman Catholic families. I was nineteen, and I had a cold. I took off my wedding ring afterwards to show it around. My mother screamed. "That's terribly unlucky!" Perhaps it was. Leigh was dear and sweet, and I adored him, but I had not the slightest idea how to be a barrister's wife I wanted parties, and dances and gaiety. I wanted life! Poor Leigh. What did we have in common? I could never speak to him about my feelings as a woman. Or my passion to be an actress. When he found out I was already enrolled at RADA, the newly opened Royal Academy of Dramatic Art, he wanted me to leave. Then I became pregnant.

*Pause. Lights change. She is again the young **VIVIEN**, writing in her diary, at the dressing table.*

VIVIEN: 12TH October, 1933. Dear Diary, today I had a baby. A girl. Suzanne. It was very messy. I don't think I'll do that again.

Lights up, the present.

VIVIEN: I didn't know how to be maternal. Leigh and my mother were shocked at my lack of interest in my own child, but we had a cook, a maid and a nanny, who looked after her, much better than I could! Suzanne was a novelty to me. Like my marriage. I could feel Leigh's resentment, so I took his first name as my stage name.

She pours herself water, and takes some pills, then pours herself another large gin.

VIVIEN: The suddenness of fame. In a way, I was quite prepared. I had been dreaming of it for years. The play was called "The Mask of Virtue." They wanted someone to play a prostitute who masquerades as an innocent girl, luring a French aristocrat into a disgraceful marriage. My agent told me she had to be spectacularly beautiful. I was always embarrassed when people spoke of my beauty. The Nuns taught me to dislike compliments. I remember walking into the audition room and it was filled with beautiful faces. The director came out, looked around the room, went back into my agent and said: "If Vivien Leigh is the girl dressed in black, she has the part!" We opened at the Ambassadors theatre on 15th May 1935. *(She speaks as if reading from a newspaper)* New 19 year old star! Vivien Leigh shines

in new play. Young actress a triumph. New star to win all London... Alexander Korda was in the audience. He had already employed me in some very forgettable films.
(In Korda's accent) "Vivien, I don't believe you have star quality..." That night he came backstage, full of apologetic charm. "Even a Hungarian can make a mistake!" He offered me a film contract on the spot. I was on my way. Life would never be the same again.

Lights change. On the screen is a Press Conference. Voices of reporters.
*Lights on the young **VIVIEN** who turns this way and that for the press photographers. She is sweet and beguiling.*

VIVIEN: You can be happy combining a career and marriage, but it's arduous. It's not simply fame in a night that I have to deal with. I manage a husband, a house in Mayfair with a small staff of servants and of course, an eighteen month old daughter. I leave the house by six or seven thirty every morning when I am filming, and if I am rehearsing and playing at the theatre as well, I have to run the house by a sort of correspondence course with my housekeeper. In the last few weeks, my husband and I hardly saw each other at all. That was rather awful of course, but he is as much interested in my acting as I am and he is very nice to put up with it... How Leigh must have cringed when he read that!

On the screen a photo of Covent Garden. Music.

VIVIEN: The night I became a star, after a party at the Savoy, we danced until four, then Leigh and I taxied to Fleet Street for the morning papers. I was the toast of London. Anything was possible now. With my husband at my side, in the damp grey light of early morning, I stood shivering in my evening gown, and I could see in my mind's eye, the marquee lights shining. Laurence Olivier and Vivien Leigh. On the same bill. And I made a promise to myself. Someday. Someday, I am going to marry Laurence Olivier.

*Fade. Lights up. We are back in the dressing room. **VIVIEN** stands for a moment looking into the past. She holds her head in pain.*

VIVIEN: The hound of Hell is pursuing me and coming ever closer. Bobbie Helpmann said to Jack: "You simply must calm her down!" Irene Selznick sent me to a doctor she knows. I'm sure she has told Jack I am mad. Poor Jack. Soon I shall be too much for him. As I was for you, Larry. I'm so unreliable. Sometimes suicidal, manic, down, up. I don't think Jack ever equated my erratic behaviour with madness. He looked so worried today as we drove to the surgery of that awful Doctor. He bravely and loyally insisted I can be a marvellous example to everyone, a figure of hope and encouragement to thousands. Thank you very much but I have no wish to be some sort of dotty Florence Nightingale! I just want to be well again…

Lights dim, until we can only see her face.

VIVIEN: I was right not to trust that doctor. He gave me another series of shock treatments. Electro-convulsive therapy. Jack sat outside and heard my screams.

*Sound: Jagged, relentless, noise. Blue, flashing light. **VIVIEN** holds her face in a silent scream. Lights fade.*

End Scene Two

Act One
Scene Three

*A day later. **VIVIEN** enters. She is jumpy, and nervous, unable to sit still. She pours herself a drink, examines her face in the mirror.*

VIVIEN: Yesterday I had one more treatment with Irene's doctor, and again last night I played Paola with a rotten headache. And this awful burn on my forehead. "You have the courage of a Lion," Jack said. Not today. Poor Jack. Now he's seen me at my worst. Everyone is worried about me. Somehow I manage to go onstage and give a performance. And no-one knows that I am mad. *(She lights a cigarette and paces)* I speak to you as if you are still by my side. At least this way I have your full attention. Something I haven't had for quite some time. But whenever I try to put my thoughts to paper I lose myself in memory. If I could only hide somewhere in the past. The present is so full of fear. The future unthinkable... Jack says what I have done to you in the Press could be regarded as collusion and no divorce may be allowed. I suspect he has been talking to you. Do you still have some concern for my mental health? You could hardly expect your letter to be very good for my nerves. I have completely come apart. Jack seems really to love me. That, at least, is good for my self-esteem. It's surely fate we have met again. Jack was with us in our golden days. He confessed to me once that he always wanted to find a love like ours. I admit I did take the first step towards him. "When are we going to make love properly?" I asked him. Properly. One of my favourite words for what I really approve of. But Jack is a proud man. Painful for him to see me tortured by my love for you- I'm sure you're relieved he now has the responsibility of looking after your mad wife. I hear you invited the Press into your house for a drink. What a very grand Larry gesture! Of course, you charmed them completely. "I'm sorry I have been so uncooperative..." I can see the performance. They came out knowing no more they had before. *(Pause)* I suppose I have done wrong. Jill Esmond, in similar circumstances, behaved with much more discretion.

Lights change. Music. On the screen another dressing room. Voices. The young ***VIVIEN*** *stands in the spotlight.*

VIVIEN: I meet you again after a matinee performance of your Romeo. You were fearless, and your magnetism leapt across the stage. I have to go backstage.

“I’m Vivien Leigh. I just had to tell you how marvellous you were.”
“I remember you. Thank you. And thank you for that soft little kiss on the back of my neck.”
“I’m glad you noticed.”
“Shall we have lunch?”
“I will have to check my diary.”
“The Ivy? Tomorrow?”
“I just happen to be free.”
I was very disappointed when you brought John Gielgud! You were much wittier than I expected. So charming. You told very funny stories about yourself and your black eyes shone. You dazzled me.
(In Larry’s voice) “Theatre and the classics are all that matter. Film is just a way of making money…”
“Then I must play the classics.”
(In Gielgud’s voice) “How would you like to play the Queen in Richard II for a week in Oxford?”
That luncheon changed my thinking. You had already begun to guide my career… *(Reciting)* “The King has come…” I loved my first experience of the classics…

On the screen, the funeral of King George.

VIVIEN: King George died that year. 20th January, 1936. Jill gave you a son. You called him Tarquin. I had influenza in June, which left me with a constant cough. I was terribly thin, but that didn't stop me smoking. *(She smokes and coughs)* Korda called me into his office.

"You smoke too much, Vivien."

"Dear Alex, you smoke like a chimney yourself."

"You're too thin. I'm worried about you."

"And you over-indulge yourself in every way."

"Would you for once in your life listen to me?"

"I'm listening."

"Larry is apparently happily married."

"Are you warning me about smoking or Larry, dear Alex?"

A few days later he cast us as lovers in Fire over England! We began to spend all our time together. You became my entire world. Everyone noticed, including Korda, but he didn't interfere. European filmmakers were always more tolerant of the private lives of their actors. When you went off to Capri with Jill after the film was finished, I didn't know what to do with myself. Leigh and I had planned to go to the continent for the summer, but at the last moment he couldn't get away so he allowed me to go with his dear friend, Oswald Frewen. As chaperone. I didn't tell him I was determined to see you and Jill in Capri. Poor Oswald wondered what on earth he had got himself into. It was rather like a scene from "Private

Lives." The three of us greeted each other like old friends. No-one would have suspected anything. Beautiful Capri. There, you and I knew we were hopelessly in love…

Lights Fade to darkness. On the screen a picture of Edward and Wallis Simpson.
*Music. Lights up on the dressing room. The older **VIVIEN**.*

VIVIEN: It was the year for romance. We all waited expectantly as Edward II fought for his throne and the woman he loved. I identified with Mrs. Simpson. I could easily have been a King's mistress. You were my prince of players, on your way to becoming a King. I remember talking with Noel Coward about us. I worried that if we divorced our spouses, the scandal might ruin your career. One week later, Edward abdicated. I wept. You went home to Jill and I lay sleepless beside Leigh. Oh such guilt. I convinced myself we couldn't possibly run away together. Gertrude realised what was happening, and we had angry scenes. She was less concerned about an affair, than a divorce. There is a passage in Gone with the Wind. Scarlett is happy her mother is dead so that she can't see what a bad girl Scarlett has become. That was me. Why couldn't I feel maternal love for my daughter, Suzanne? Why couldn't I live up to my Faith like my mother? Why couldn't I feel desire for Leigh? I tried to be a perfect companion but I wanted only you. You were my lover, my confidant, my advisor. My God. I worshipped your talent. I saw your Hamlet fourteen times. You were the greatest actor alive. Unless I achieved greatness on stage, I would never be worthy of you. That was when I first read Gone with the Wind. I became obsessed with Scarlett O'Hara. If I played her I would gain international stardom. I would be on a more equal footing with you.

She goes to a gramophone and puts on the music from Gone With The Wind.

VIVIEN: Whenever I am depressed I put on the music from Gone with the Wind. It always makes me feel better. I was Scarlett. Margaret Mitchell might have been describing me.

She listens and gently waltzes around the room. Lights fade. On the screen behind, the burning of Atlanta from the film. The young ***VIVIEN*** *appears in the spotlight, now wearing a black hat.*

VIVIEN: "My God, you are Scarlett!" Myron Selznick says when I first meet him. You were in Los Angeles, making Wuthering Heights. It was insane to go there for five days, but I was reckless, desperate to see you. Despite the rough crossing in the Queen Mary, throwing up all the time, despite flying from New York to Los Angeles, I'm terrified of flying, I was completely happy. I was coming to you. If I was cast as Scarlett we would be together. Myron Selznick, being a clever theatrical agent, took you and I to dinner on the night of the burning of Atlanta. David O. Selznick had begun filming Gone with the Wind, even though he still had not found his Scarlet. Myron kept us at dinner until I could make my entrance at the height of the blaze...

Lights are red on her face, reflecting the burning flames. Music.

VIVIEN: David O. Selznick looks like a giant on the high observation platform. The stairs shake as I climb. I'm dressed in black, and keep my head down, holding my hat.
When I reach the top, I whip is off, and my hair blows wildly.

You sad the flames of Atlanta lit up my face. "Here genius," Myron announces. "Meet your Scarlett O'Hara..." Selznick gasps.

*Music swells. Flames on screen. Blackout. Lights up in dressing room. The older **VIVIEN** switches off the music. As she talks she takes off her suit and puts on a dressing gown.*

VIVIEN: I had won the role of a lifetime. That success reached out and enveloped me for the rest of my days. The biggest star in the biggest film. You were amazed, impressed and furious. I was better on film than you. I understood that you make love to the camera. You were always more interested in showing off...

She stands silently smoking and drinking.

VIVIEN: I'm sure Jill knew after Capri that she was losing you. We were so wildly in love we couldn't hide our feelings. One day she came to see me. She said she needed to talk. She looked quite desperate. I knew she wanted me to let you go. I pretended not to have a care in the world, and I chatted on gaily about nothing. Jill lost courage. We never spoke about it. Anyway, it was too late. I had been invited to join the

Old Vic. Ophelia to your Hamlet in Elsinore. Once we left London, we threw off all restraint.

Lights dim to a spot. Sound of wind, rain, and sea. Thunder. On screen, Kronborg Castle.

VIVIEN: It is freezing. *(She coughs)* I can't get warm. We are going to perform Hamlet in the courtyard of Kronborg Castle. It is Denmark's wettest summer for twenty three years. The sea crashes against the walls, and we rehearse with umbrellas, against the heavy rain and thunder. You are wrapped in towels as you do your soliloquies, shouting over the rain and the sea and a chorus of steam hammers from the shipyards next door. Jill stands expressionless, watching you and I rehearse our scenes. She is soaked but she won't move! The sky is dark and furious, and the wind makes it impossible to be heard. I have such a small voice and I'm worried that you will be disappointed in me. Where is the sun? I am so cold. I hate the cold.

The Lights change to dressing room.

VIVIEN: I have always lived in the sun. In your golden sunlight. The Times sent a reviewer to Denmark. Your Hamlet was wonderful. I showed promise. Was that an omen for our future? *(She holds* *her head)* My head still hurts. When Jack took me back for another treatment today, my head was aching so much, I thought I would go mad.

She stands in a spotlight. She is outside the Doctor's surgery, in a very nervous state. Her voice is hard and rasping, her eyes cold.

VIVIEN: No, Jack I will not go in! (Coldly) There's really no point in your trying to talk sense into me, as you call it, because I have made up my mind that I will not have another treatment with that man! He is a monster! What could you possibly know about my condition? Who are you to advise me? If I let him, that monster will make me into a fucking vegetable! Is that what you want? Is that what you all want? Don't look at me with those sad, cow eyes. I don't want or need your sympathy. It's my fucking brain, Jack! My head hurts! Dear God, how my head hurts! I have never felt this way after Dr. Conachy's treatment. Oh, stop looking at me like that! Take your hands off me! *(She begins to scream loudly)* Get away from me! I have to speak to Dr. Conachy! I insist on speaking with Dr. Conachy in London! Can't you understand? He brought me back to life before! He will bring me back again! I must speak to him!

Lights change back to the dressing room.

VIVIEN: The moment I heard Conachy's voice it calmed me. I could speak quite sensibly. He made them agree not to give me any more shock treatments. They will try medication. But Irene's doctor warned me the manic phase will last longer than usual… After Denmark we escaped to Venice for a holiday. It was July, and Venice shone. We stayed at a hotel on the Grand Canal. We fed the pigeons, strolled hand in hand in the sunlight, walked in the moonlight. When we returned to London we moved into together. Leigh behaved very decently. I think he always believed I would come back to him. You had left your wife and son and I had deserted my husband and daughter. I was deeply anxious. But there was no turning back.

Vivien sits down at her dressing table and begins putting on her makeup.

End Act One

Act Two

Scene One

Time, June 1960. The living room of Vivien and Larry's house at Notley, England. It has been denuded of much furniture. A table and chairs downstage. Packing cases.

VIVIEN, in a suit, stands at the French windows, looking out. It is raining.

VIVIEN: And so we were married. 31st August, 1940. One minute after midnight, when the license became legally valid, after a pre-wedding party with Kate Hepburn and Garson Kannin, we all drove a hundred miles down to Santa Barbara, and married in the living room of old friends. It was a short service. Three minutes. When we kissed, the Judge shouted, "Bingo!"

A pause. She looks out at the rain.

VIVIEN: I have come back to Notley. Equity called a Theatre strike in New York and Duel of Angels has closed for a month, until we open in Los Angeles, and do a tour. Since you have been showing Notley to buyers, I've come back to collect my things. I feel in my heart this is the last time I shall be here. It is raining and the Thames is shrouded in mist. The gardens are in a dreadful state. Rather like myself. The house is so empty. Silent. Like a death. We are stripping away our lives. Only the ghosts will remain. Ghosts of golden days. When love lived here.

She moves around the room. Listlessly she pours herself a drink, then sits down at the table, taking up pen and paper.

VIVIEN: I still haven't replied to your letter. My darling, if you knew how many crumpled bits of memory I have thrown away. Wasted words. You will never hear. I thought at Notley I would know exactly what to say. I planned to leave the letter on the mantelpiece strategically placed between your two Oscars. Oscar's gone. So are you. *(She throws down the pen; she gets up again restlessly and moves to the mantelpiece)* You were so consumed with jealousy when I received an Academy Award for Scarlett. You refused to talk about it. Until of course you got two of your own. Henry V and Hamlet. They all sat together like bookends. *(She wanders around restlessly)* My farewell letter to you would sit so nicely and fittingly between them. What are the right words? You don't want the truth! You want me to let you go from this untenable relationship as you called it, with dignity and grace. Excuse me, if I don't feel particularly gracious or dignified!

A pause. She lights a cigarette (or pours a drink) and paces.

VIVIEN: The reporters were waiting when I came out of Customs at Heathrow. Thank God, Bobby Helpmann and Peter Wyngarde were with me.

Lights change and she is facing the Press, puffing nervously n her cigarette.

VIVIEN: "I thought I was going to see Larry at his Theatre, but he phoned me and said he believed it best not to meet right now. He said he would see me later but there are no definite arrangements..."

Lights change back to Notley. She is trying not to cry.

VIVIEN: I was in a terrible state after you refused to see me. Gertrude had to call Conachy at two in the morning. I feel slightly better now. I think I am behaving normally. I take so many pills, I'm never quite sure. Why the hell won't you see me? If I could only meet you face to face and look into your eyes. I was your Queen! How dare you dismiss me so easily like some handmaiden? How dare you?

Pause

She goes to the gramophone and put on a record. Waltz music from Gone with the Wind. She listens and then gently waltzes around the room. Stops. Music continues under.

VIVIEN: How much I disliked Notley when you first showed it to me. I saw only a 13th Century stone Abbey with huge, very cold and draughty rooms. But you loved it. Henry II, Henry VIII, and Cardinal Wolsey all stayed here. And of course, Notley had been endowed by Henry V. It was destiny, you said. You should have walked around in scabbard and sword. The Lord of the Abbey. I gave in because I always wanted to please you. Then I never wanted to leave. I never thought I would leave...

She lights a cigarette. Turns off the Music. Paces around the room.

VIVIEN: Ronald Colman offered us his schooner for the honeymoon. We climbed aboard at four A.M in the dawn light and sailed towards Catalina Island. I was Mrs. Laurence Olivier... The Press were calling us America's most famous lovers. Curious, since we are both British. *(Pause)* War had broken out. I remember we were on another yacht. With Douglas Fairbanks. All huddled round the radio. September 3rd 1939. Britain and France were at war with Germany. George Cukor suggested we do Romeo and Juliet. Our first and final appearance on stage in America before returning to Europe and the war. The publicity was extraordinary. "See the great lovers in person!" And worse. "See real lovers make love in public!" We were lovers on and offstage, so passionately in love we devoured each other. Everyone in the company could see. It was overwhelming. They said you were different with me. You laughed more: Does Joan make you laugh? I can't remember the last time I laughed out loud with sheer joy. The theatre in New York was only meant for concerts, impossible to be heard without shouting. I was terrified no-one would hear me. They gave us microphones, but when you came on, Larry, you were so loud they had to turn the sound down. So no-one did hear me. Noel Coward threw us at party. "Darlings, how brave of you to come!" "Much scenery. No play," Brooks Atkinson in the New York Times. "Miss Leigh and Laurence Olivier make a spectacular personal appearance of Heathcliff and

Scarlett O'Hara rather than as an earnest impersonation of the star-crossed lovers." We closed in two weeks. There were queues around the block demanding their money back. In a very grand Larry gesture you ran out and threw money at them! I was exhausted. Voice lessons four times a week, trying to get my voice down, so tired of people saying it was too light. I was the most famous woman in the world, but it wasn't enough. I was in love with a genius. Sometimes I felt such panic…

A pause

Jack has remained in New York. I don't know if he wants to be with me anymore. I would understand if he didn't. In my manic phase I am not very nice. He should have seen the signs that weekend he came to visit us in Connecticut. Was it the beginning? Do you remember Katherine Cornell's house at Sneden's landing? That converted barn? We were so depressed there. We had lost all our savings on the play. There was a war on, and we were in a sort of limbo. I was drinking far too much and very restless…

Lights change as she retreats into the past. On screen we see the House.

VIVIEN: The evening had started so pleasantly. Just the three of us. You reading by the fire, studying for your pilot's license. Jack and I are playing Chinese Checkers. Chinker Checks as we called it. Such a silly game but we played it all the time, and I loved it. Then suddenly I can't concentrate. I keep drumming my fingers impatiently on the table. Edgy, nervous. I seem to be standing outside myself and I can't get back inside. Jack looks at me, puzzled by the change in me.

"You're not playing properly..."

"Don't tell me how to play!"

You are stuck in your book and don't hear. Or don't want to hear. "How dare you invite yourself down here and then cheat at Chinker Checks!" It was as if something had taken hold of me.

"I'm not cheating..." Jack is so bewildered.

"What the hell is going on?" You look up from your book, and I am terrified at the expression in your eyes. I can't stop crying. I'm screaming at Jack "Don't try and come between us! We've been together for four years now and nobody's going to fucking come between us!"

I'd begun using quite a few four letter words they didn't teach at the Convent. You taught me those, Larry.

Lights change. The Present.

VIVIEN: Jack was gone the next morning before we got up. I didn't see him again for years. The beginning of the sudden flare-ups. Sometimes I don't remember what I've done. I am always terribly sorry afterwards. I've written so many letters of apology over the years. One of the demands of my condition. Forever apologising. Was I too terrible? Did I flash my twot again? Did I remove all my clothes in front of everyone? And curse like a Navvy? But please tell me I didn't hurt anyone. Physically? Did I hit you? You see its part of my condition. I often don't remember what I've done. From what I've heard it is a blessing I don't remember. I am sorry. I'm sorry. I'm sorry. It's remarkable how generous and forgiving most of my friends can be. Sorry, sorry, sorry. I am so very sorry. Yet I can't write sorry to you, Larry. Perhaps because I know you don't forgive. Or won't. Or can't... After the honeymoon, and the disaster of Romeo and Juliet, we decided to go home, to England. But first we filmed Lady Hamilton for Korda in Los Angeles. Your Lord Nelson would boost American sympathy for Britain, and hopefully bring America into the war. Lady Hamilton. In every frame we are falling more in love. Gertrude brought the children over because we were afraid to leave them in

London. Tarquin looked so thin and very pale. His legs were not growing properly and Jill was taking him for treatment in New York. I placed Suzanne in a convent. Not much older than I was, then the Mother Superior politely said she had to leave. They feared kidnapping threats. I suspect it was because I was a divorced woman. So Mother had to stay on with Suzanne. Separated from Ernest in London and unable to keep his roving eyes on a tight leash. Gertrude was not happy.

Lights change. On a screen, a devastated London.

VIVIEN: Scarlett O'Hara stands in a hotel room with blown out windows. London is in total darkness. Like Tara, after the war.

The sound of bombs falling. Sirens. Lights flashing across a hotel room.

VIVIEN: Oh God, Larry, do you hear the sirens? The sky is red. Blood red. The bombs are falling. Windows breaking. Glass shattering. Larry, hold me. Hold me... hold me tightly...

The lights change and we are back at Notley. Vivien is crying.

VIVIEN: Please hold me, I am so frightened. None of this seems real. I will wake up in the morning, here at Notley and you will be beside me…

Lights change and she is back in London. The sound of planes overhead and bombs.

VIVIEN: I thought war would give me courage. It doesn't. Hollywood seems a lifetime away. London is depressing. This war is depressing. Everything seems futile. The West End is almost dark. Each day more sad news. The loss of friends. I can't sleep. I haven't slept for days. I read Dickens through the night. Or I lie awake listening to the planes overhead. I close my eyes and tell myself it is the audience clapping. But the clapping won't stop. The whole world seems under a cloud of dark fear. Everywhere black holes where buildings once were. Little Stanhope St- gone.

Lights change. She is back at Notley.

VIVIEN: All gone. Larry gone. Hold me, Larry… I am a wartime wife trying to fill in the days. The attacks of nerves come more frequently. I am far too thin, with a constant cough. You're away so much. I wave you goodbye in the morning, as you set off on your motorbike for lessons at the sea plane base. You never did become the hero you wanted to be. You were a terrible pilot. You smashed three planes; I know you're worried about me. I see it in your eyes. I want to play Katherine in your Henry V but Selznick won't let me. He's furious because he's offered film roles to me for a year and I've refused them all. My country needs me, I told him. I can't leave you. I won't. You suggest I tour in Shaw's Doctor's Dilemma. The great man will see my performance and surely want me to play his Cleopatra in Gabriel Pascal's film of Anthony and Cleopatra. The great man never came to see the play. So I went to see him. Vivien determined to get her own way again. Beware of what you want for you will surely get it.

Lights change.

VIVIEN: Binkie Beaumont invites me to Shaw's flat in Whitehall Court. I don't talk about Cleopatra, but for Mr. Shaw that afternoon, I am a Persian kitten. Cleopatra is only sixteen in his play. I have never acted better. Mr. Shaw has a glint in his eye.
"You know what you ought to do is play Cleopatra!"
"Do you really think so? Would I be good enough?"
"Oh don't worry. The part is fool proof. You don't need to be an actress!"

Lights change.

VIVIEN: On 12th July, just six weeks after the Allies invasion of Normandy, the cameras begin to roll on Caesar and Cleopatra at Denham Studios, with Claude Rains as Caesar. Britain's most expensive picture. Pity poor Rank, said Mr. Shaw. The summer has turned cold. I run from the warmth of a small electric fire in my dressing room to a freezing cold open field. Wearing filmy gowns, and pretending to swelter in an Egyptian summer. Gabriel Pascal works so slowly! I'm frustrated with his pedantic, unimaginative direction! He makes me run up and down Memphis Palace, while I beat a slave. CUT! Pascal doesn't like the lighting. CUT!!! Pascal wants a long shot. CUT! CUT! CUT! I run to the throne, throwing my arms up! "I am a Queen at last- a real, real Queen! Cleopatra the Queen!"

Lights come up at Notley.

VIVIEN: I slipped on the polished floor. *(Pause)* No bones broken. I went into the film knowing I was carrying your child. The doctor warned me against it. I was so well and strong and happy, so sure of your love, I wouldn't listen. At long last, we would have a family. I could be a mother again. This time I would appreciate my child. Your child. It would bind us tightly together. I smiled bravely and went on filming, but somewhere inside me, a light had gone out. The cameras picked it up. "Oh well. There'll be plenty more where that one came from!"

End Scene One

ACT TWO
Scene Two

Time continued. Scene Notley.
*A dishevelled **VIVIEN** is lying on the floor in a foetal position, just in a skirt and blouse. After a moment, she sits up and looks around as though not sure where she is as she talks, she is in and out of the past, in and out of reality…*

VIVIEN: "I've been to a marvellous party. I must say the fun was intense!" We are the two most beautiful people in the world. Ours is the most scandalous and glorious love story of all time. We are golden, magical. The hope of the war years, they say. Everyone wants to read about us, see our pictures in the papers, and meet us. Every weekend, Notley is crowded with visitors. So much laughter and joy. *(Sing/talks)* "I went to a marvellous party..."

A pause

VIVIEN: I lost my baby... One day in the middle of filming Caesar and Cleopatra I suddenly stopped acting and began shouting at my dresser for no reason. They dragged me screaming to my dressing room. I didn't go back to the set for six weeks. Of course, I wrote letters of apology to everyone. You said my hysteria was due to the loss of the baby, and overwork. I don't believe you took my mood seriously until the night I start abusing you. Such cruel, hurtful words. I attack you physically. Accusing, paranoid, shrieking and wild. Sobbing on the floor, hysterical, like a lost child. You stare at me as if I am a stranger. The next day, you tell me what I had done. I had no memory of it. That was the most awful part. No, I won't see a Doctor! Larry, I'm not having a nervous collapse! I can't bear you to think less of me... The golden couple can't be less than perfect. The angels have sprinkled so much gold dust on us...

Lights change. Music. Sound of cheering and celebration. On the screen newsreel footage of VE Day.

VIVIEN: The war is over! We are numb with relief. Gertrude brings Suzanne back to London. She is thirteen, cheerful and good mannered. *(Pause)* I have nothing to say to her. She will be much better off living with her Father. Leigh and I have become such good friends since the war. He has never blamed me. I can rely on him. I know I seek his approval. We needed money, so you planned to direct me in Thornton Wilder's "Skin of Our Teeth." Selznick took me to court.

"Miss Leigh is an exotic plant which must be exposed widely."

"I am a British Citizen, sir! I face possible drafting into a war factory if I don't act on the stage."

I win the case. Jack came backstage one night when we were trying out in Bristol. Fresh from his divorce to the actress, Jan Sterling. He didn't mention what had happened the last time we met. I made him promise to keep in touch. The play is a London sensation. Such a wonderful opening night! With the War over, glamour had returned to the West End. "Lovely performance from Miss Leigh as Sabina, the hired girl, half dabchick and half dragon fly." That was surprisingly generous of James Agate. Considering you punched him because he was late for the curtain. We are the Oliviers. The golden couple. We glitter and dazzle for the next few years. But I lose more weight. This terrible cough. Either exhausted or exhilarated. One night on stage, feverish and strange, I cough up blood. Tuberculosis. Not a romantic disease. I am no Camille. But it explains why I am behaving so strangely. The Doctor wants me to go into a Sanatorium for six months. Perhaps a year. NO! Never! Nothing will persuade me to do that! Even you, Larry, can't persuade me! You see, all that time, I had a secret fear I was going mad. I have a horror of Sanatoriums. That would be like you sending me to a lunatic asylum! I promise to stay quietly living at Notley! Yes, I will agree to give up the stage for a year! Four months in bed during a cold, bitter winter. And yet that is when I truly came to love Notley. I can see the garden from my bedroom window The Thames drifting through the fields and woods. The garden we planted begins to flourish in the Spring. I love Notley as much as you. Yet even there I had another attack. I began to see a pattern. For a few days before, I'm very nervous, laughing too loudly, speaking quickly. Then comes the madness. Screaming and crying, sometimes for hours. The terror in your eyes makes me worse. Physical illness you could cope with. But madness? I know you still love me but now I make you anxious. You're working so hard. Driving yourself on to reach the heights, in Oedipus and Richard III. That season is your triumph. Every night crowds of girls outside the stage door, screaming. "Larry! We want Larry!" The theatre has never seen anything like it. Your Lear makes you England's greatest contemporary actor. You are the King. God has touched you on the shoulder. You are still the centre of my world but I am not part of your new triumphs. Can I ever reach the same heights? When I am well, I nag you to direct me in Antigone. I need something to compare. The Press say I have become a great tragic actress, but afterwards the emotions of that role stay with me. I can't let them go. You seem so removed. Like a stranger. I am afraid. You refuse to cast me as Ophelia in your film of Hamlet. How can I be too old at thirty three, you're forty for God's sake! Jean Simmons is eighteen! People said she looked like me!

Music. Pomp and ceremony. On screen Buckingham Palace.

VIVIEN: You have bleached your hair blonde for Hamlet. You are wearing Ralph Richardson's vest, because he wore the same vest when he was knighted. You step forward. I am left standing alone in the Grand Hall of Buckingham Palace. You walk up the long aisle, and kneel before King George. He touches you lightly on each shoulder. Rise. Laurence Olivier.

Knight Bachelor. At forty, the youngest actor ever to receive such an honour. Sir Laurence and Lady Olivier. The golden couple now really are royalty. When we toured the Old Vic Company to Australia, we were treated very like the Royal family. Ovations, grand receptions, tributes. In the fresh air, the wide open spaces, the light, can we rediscover our passion? Be like young lovers again? Then we meet Peter Finch. Sensual and sexy. Strong and funny. You immediately invite him to join the company. The sort of man I am always attracted to.

Pause. Lights change. Music.

VIVIEN: I wanted to play Blanche DuBois in A Streetcar Named Desire as much as I had wanted to play Scarlett. Jessica Tandy played it in New York, but you direct me in London. I play Blanche for eight months. Was I all right? Am I mad to be doing it? I know it's dangerous. I know. Every night I'm touching the darkness! The darkness I have for so long tried to run from. After the final scene, where Blanche is taken away to a mental hospital, I can't stop shaking. My lips are trembling. Blanche tipped me into madness. Then the film, with Brando. We return to America. Nine years ago we were disgraced lovers. Now we are Sir Laurence and Lady Olivier. "Lady Olivier how does it feel to be back?"

"Her Ladyship is fucking bored with such formality she prefers to be known as Vivien Leigh." Charlie Feldman, the film's producer, looks distinctly nervous. "Vivien, does Larry read you his lines in bed?"

"Yes, it's perfectly wonderful! He puts me to sleep..."

Lights change. ***VIVIEN*** *for a moment becomes Blanche. Pacing nervously...*

VIVIEN: I understand Blanche. She is a woman with everything stripped away. I understand her struggle. Sometimes when I am depressed I feel I have gone down to hell. I have strange, almost overwhelming sexual fantasies. I walk along the street and I want to accost a stranger. Anyone. Take him home and seduce him. A compulsion so strong, it takes all my strength to resist. I am afraid to be left alone. Once, a taxi driver. A delivery man. Rough trade. The idea of having sex with someone who is working class. It would ease the guilt. No, if I give into these dreadful fantasies, the guilt will be far worse. I'm not like that! I've always been known for my taste and elegance. My fastidiousness. How can I degrade myself! I can't talk to anyone about this. I certainly can't tell you!

God help me! I am going mad! I want to feel innocent again! Pure…

Lights change.

VIVIEN: It was my brilliant suggestion we do Anthony and Cleopatra, and Caesar and Cleopatra together. Shaw, Shakespeare, the crowning jewels in the Festival of Britain. Then I am afraid I will let you down in the Shakespeare. The cast can see I am having problems, but they are kind, and on my side. They whisper that you have changed. You are unapproachable. Is it my fault? Or having climbed Olympus, are you now different to mere mortals? The closer we get to opening, the worse my nerves. I feel terror. The critics love it. "Miss Leigh is at the heyday of her power, a cool enchantress…" Others say I am holding you back. Who is this Kenneth Tynan? The most talented critic of his generation. No, he's callous. Self-confident. Loves you, hates me. He viciously attacks me. My neck's too long, my hands too big, my voice too small! No matter how I work on my voice, the critics say it is too lightweight for the classics! You defend me from Tynan, but I know you secretly admire him. He flatters your vanity. You become close friends, even though Tynan always sees me as some sort of parasite, feeding off your talent. One night I walk off at the curtain call because you had accidentally spattered my gown with blood. The first time I ever rowed with you in public. You become more remote. People are talking, whispering behind my back, about my illness. "She's seeing a doctor! A Psychiatrist!" And you are afraid I am going mad. Even an Oscar for Streetcar doesn't help. I'm nearing forty! I'm not young anymore. I am terrified at the thought of losing my youth. I hate the young. I am jealous of them. So I drink to numb the pain. I'm happy and I'm sad and I cry for no good reason. I keep drinking. And watch you crumbling under the burden, as my attacks become more frequent, more disturbing. We are losing our love. So many indiscretions. We thought we could survive anything. Even my affair with Peter Finch, when I told you I didn't love you anymore. The look on your face. I didn't mean it. I just wanted us to be what we were. There can be no question of divorce. We are the Oliviers. The golden ones. If you left me, Larry, I would do something dreadful. You must never leave me.

Lights change. VIVIEN is now falling into madness.

VIVIEN: You put me on a plane with Peter Finch and he and I go off to Ceylon to make Elephant Walk. I'm only doing it for the money. The warm, sensuous heat reminds me of India, and the world of my childhood. So many memories. So hot. The deep blue sea. Emerald green forests. It's so unbearably hot. Nothing seems real. I don't like the director, it's so hot. I am afraid. I can't remember my lines. I never have trouble learning lines. I can't sleep. I walk around alone at night, along the beaches. I can't be still. I have to keep going. Where am I going? Where am I? The director says I look tired and old in the rushes. So, what's wrong with that! At least you are here Larry. Of course I know who you are, Peter! No you're Larry. Tell me you're Larry. I have to do a scene with two huge snakes around my neck. It takes all day. Dreadful cobras twisting around. Cold, icy, slimy creatures with evil eyes that takes my soul. I am lost. I am so lost. Catch me, I am falling. If you don't catch me, Larry, I shall fall forever into the darkness. Take these fucking things off me! *(She screams and begins to shudder uncontrollably. Sobbing.)* Holy Mother of God, pray for me. St. Therese pray for me. *(She begins to talk in a Southern accent, becoming Blanch Dubois)* Thank you. I have always depended on the kindness of strangers. No! I don't wish to be sedated! Where are you taking me? Why are we on a plane? I have never liked flying. You must know that I am terrified of flying. *(She starts trying to rip her clothes off)* Let me go, you fucking monsters. Let me out of here! Let me go. Before I start screaming fire! Fire! Fire! Fire!

She falls.
Blackout

End Scene Two

ACT TWO
Scene Three

On the screen reads a headline: VIVIEN LEIGH RETURNS TO AUSTRALIA!
Newsreel footage. Applause. Cheers and bravos which slowly fade…
Lights up. Another dressing room. Much the same as the one before, although less opulent. Dressing table is downstage left. A door centre stage leads to the corridor and the stage. A door downstage right is the bathroom.

***VIVIEN** in a dressing gown sits at the table, writing on a postcard. She drinks and smokes. She finishes writing.*

VIVIEN: Last night was so wonderful. I need to share it with you. So many moments I still want to share.

Of course I think of you all the time here in Australia. *(She reads aloud what she has written)* My dearest Larry, I am writing this after a tremendous Melbourne opening of Duel of Angels. It is good to be back in Australia. The wonderful light. I think of you, and our time here. Love to Joan. *(Pause)* And the baby… *(She stops reading)* You held the child up for the Press and said none of the worldly honours you had ever achieved could equal this joy.

VIVIEN is silent for a moment then continues reading.

VIVIEN: And my love as always to you, dear Larry. *(She puts down the postcard)* So, at least I have written you a postcard. I never did finish that letter to you. After the divorce, there didn't seem any point. I left that courtroom with as much composure as I could muster, and then sat back in the rear seat of a Rolls, and sobbed. It all seemed terribly unreal. A future without you. It was as if you had died.

Pause. She surveys her dressing room.

VIVIEN: Another dressing room. They all look very much alike. So we are back in Melbourne. Just like '48. I keep expecting you to dash in the door. We are touring with the Old Vic, three plays including Duel of Angels. It's not the same. No-one really thinks Jack compares to you. I still talk to you, you see, as if you are here. All the thoughts I could never put down on paper. All the words I never said. If you could hear me, you would laugh and tell me I am mad. And I am. How can I blame you, Larry? You'd had enough. After my breakdown on "Elephant Walk", in that hospital in Surrey, they kept me sedated, packed me in ice to lower my body temperature no visitors, not even you. I thought I was in a lunatic asylum. I used to scream for help. No-one came. When they finally let me go home to Notley, I was calm one day, frantic another. I clung to the hope of a miracle to change things, but I only saw pity in your eyes. We stopped talking to each other. The silence was like a wall. We were to do Rattigan's Sleeping Prince. You called it "A courtier's offering" to Queen Elizabeth II in her Coronation year. It was my attempt at a return to normal life. There is a line in that play. I am forty and I have never found true love. I was forty and I didn't like it. Eva Peron died at thirty three. She was lucky. Sometimes I stood waiting to go on stage, and I would mutter insanities to myself. Yet somehow I gave a performance. When we did Twelfth Night, they lauded your Malvolio. I was lovely to look at. And in the Scottish play that cannot be named, I certainly won't say it in this dressing room, it's terribly unlucky, Tynan wrote that you shook hands with greatness. And I was niminy piminy. Everyone said he was wrong. If you were as furious to defend me as you claimed why did you invite him down to lunch and force me to be charming? Noel Coward was there, and as usual did not miss a thing. "There you both are. Eminent, successful, envied and adored, and most wretchedly unhappy." You confided to him that your life had become impossible. When we were doing Titus Andronicus, I used to swear at you under my breath. "You shit, you shit!" "Fuck you! Fuck you!" You would swear back, in between spouting poetry. Where did love go? The gold dust had turned to ashes. I think I ran away with Peter Finch because I felt I had let you down. Oh God. We were only on the train a few moments, when I pulled the emergency cord. I couldn't do it. I could not leave you behind. Leave everything you stood for in my life. I couldn't. Peter brought me back to Notley and I collapsed in hysterics. You were doing the Prince and the Showgirl with Marilyn Monroe in my role. "The Blonde Bottom" as you called her. And I was pregnant again. *(Pause)* Another miscarriage…

Through that autumn I had to fight my way back to life. I wanted to die. Then a sudden manic phase. I'd turn on you; say anything cruel to hurt you as much as I was hurting. But God does answer our prayers. I met Dr. Conachy who assured me I was not schizophrenic. I was manic depressive. For the first time I had found a doctor I trusted. You were at your most confident. The public adored you. And I was commencing electro- convulsive shock treatment…

She holds her head and shudder.

VIVIEN: You chose to do the Entertainer, and leave the world of Establishment Theatre behind. The world we had shared. Picking Joan to play your daughter. My daughter had a baby and the headlines screamed." Scarlett O'Hara is a grandmother!" I was invited to Atlanta to premier the new wide screen version of Gone with the Wind. "Scarlett, we love you," the crowd chanted. Mothers and fathers bringing their grandchildren to see Vivien Leigh. A reporter asked me what part I had played in the film. He hadn't even seen it! Another reporter asked me what film I was currently making. "The Roman Spring of Mrs. Stone- and I'm not playing the Roman Spring!" Still, it was a sad occasion. Apart from Olivia De Havilland and myself, everybody else is dead.

A pause. As she talks, Music from Gone with the Wind. Lights change.

VIVIEN: By co-incidence you were in America at the same time. You finally agreed to see me. Not quite the romantic encounter I had hoped for! You only agreed to see me with Joan at your side, and in a public place. I supposed you hoped that would make me let you go. You should know me better than that my darling. When I want something, I am determined to get it. Scarlett pursued Ashley even though he was engaged to Melanie. *(In Scarlett's voice)* "Ashley wouldn't marry Melly if he knew I loved him! How could he! There's no reason why things won't come out the way I want them-if he loves me. And I know he does!"

Lights change. On the screen: Sardi's restaurant. The loud murmur of voices. ***VIVIEN*** *stands in a spot.*

VIVIEN: We met at Sardi's. I dress very carefully. I delay my entrance to make sure you were both already seated. It was early, before curtain time and Sardi's is crowded. It is not easy to walk through that crowd to your table. All heads turn, and there you both were. Seated together. I sit down opposite. You are my husband. The great love of my life. The man I still worship. I can hardly look at Joan, the woman chosen to replace me. Nice enough. She certainly wouldn't make heads turn as I had when I walked in.

Sardi's is so crowded and noisy it's impossible to have a private conversation. Which, of course, is your intention. Then you break the news. You and Joan are to be married. You hold her hand for support and she smiles at you adoringly. The way I once did. There was nothing very much to say after that. We hurried through dinner. It all took less than an hour. Then you and the soon to be second Lady Olivier escorted the first Lady Olivier out of Sardi's and very kindly helped her into a taxi.

VIVIEN is now dressing for her performance.

VIVIEN: Two days later I was back filming Roman Spring in London and the press stopped me outside my apartment. "You know it happened this morning in New York? Do you have anything to say?" I don't know what they are talking about. "Sir Laurence and Miss Plowright were married this morning…" For a moment I think I am going to faint. Jose Quintero, the director is with me and holds my arm. I straighten up, throw back my head and give my best Scarlett O'Hara smile. "Of course I knew it and when I went to New York I wished them all the happiness in the world…"

VIVIEN puts on her dress.

VIVIEN: Emma Hamilton had a final line in the film of Lady Hamilton. Nelson is dead, and she is in prison, telling her story to her fellow prisoners, a group of prostitutes. "And then what?" One prostitute asks. "What happened after?" "There is no then," Emma replies. "There is no after..." I won't think about it today. I'll think about it tomorrow...

VO: Beginners call, Miss Leigh.

VIVIEN: *(Calls)* Coming! Jack and I spent three of the most perfectly happy weeks in Tobago. We played cards and swam. I even learned to snorkel! He held me in his arms and told me I would never be sick again. I want to believe that. Once you have crossed the abyss, always mindful of the shadows that lurk there, when you have reached the other side, surely it is possible to live again? I must believe that. Remember Robert Browning's poem "A Woman's Last Word. The final couplet went. "Must a little weep, love. And so fall asleep love. Loved by thee..." I will always think of you, Larry when I say those words. Perhaps one day I will write that letter to you. Not a farewell letter. We've said our farewells. But just to say I am sorry. *(She stands and goes to the door)* I tried to live my life with magic. Like Blanche I always believed in magic. For a few golden moments, I found it.

Lights fade as for a moment she is silhouetted in the light from the corridor as she stands in the doorway, ready to go onstage. Then she closes the door. Applause begins off.

Blackout.
End Act Two